THE PRIESTHOOD

PARAMETERS AND RESPONSIBILITIES

NEMA

BLACK MOON PUBLISHING
CINCINNATI · NEW ORLEANS · BLOOMINGTON
USA

ISBN: 978-1-890399-38-2

United States • United Kingdom • Europe • Australia • Brazil

THE Priesthood is a condition of a soul on fire with love. The Priesthood is a way of life demanded by a certain level of spiritual responsibility, a way of life that focuses action and non-action toward universal enlightenment.

Like any other course of action and non-action, the Priesthood deals with the many aspects of illusion, or Maya. However, a Priest lives to eliminate the veils of illusion for him/herself and others, to ever strive for a better approximation to truth.

In the dawning of our species, each human being was his/her own Priest, participating in the immanence of Intelligence and in the balance of nature. The Divine was ever-present in the physical world, evident in analogies of the human experience percieved in natural events. The earth, as both ocean and dry land, was Mother; living things come from Her, as children are born to women.

The Sun was the Father; plants hidden from His light became sickly and died. Thunder and lightning, volcanos, floods and hurricanes were the play or the anger of the gods. Animals, trees, stones, and places had spirits animating them.

The main emphasis at history's beginning was the Earth Mother—symbol of fertility and provision, love and nurturing, death and return. At this stage, the Divine, the Human and the Natural were an organic whole. There was enough space and food for all; with the bounty of the Mother providing the necessities of life, the rich inner life of family, tribe and clan aided spiritual development without the need of a special Priesthood. Some individuals assumed the responsibility of Shaman, calling particular forces to assist in finding game, healing and fertility; rituals and feasts were tribal.

When population pressure forced tribes to move, there developed the image of the Divine as Sky-Father. Since man creates gods in his own image and likeness, the patriarchal, jealous and angry Father helped rationalize and even bless aggressive behavior.

No matter that the Caananites were there first; the Israelites were on a mission from God to take the land as promised in the Covenant. No matter that the Dravidian peoples inhabited the Indian subcontinent; the Aryans conquered in the names of Indra and Varuna, gods of the sky. With Christianity and Islam, conversion at sword-point added new refinements to conquest.

The Sky-Father religions developed the separate Priesthood.

We are in a new Aeon of Priesthood, a double Aeon of the Son and the Daughter. Today's Priesthood is a vocation to the work of unity. For some individuals, this vocation is evident

from childhood as a growing natural interest in matters of the spirit. For others, like Saul of Tarsus, the call comes in a blinding moment of revelation. Perhaps, for the larger number of the spiritually aware, the call to Priesthood manifests as a course of action arising from one's own developing wisdom gained from progress along the Initiatory path.

No matter what method, the Priesthood arises, for its practitioners, as a choice beyond choices, a natural inevitability that cannot be denied. To investigate the nature of this condition, it's necessary to trace its evolution within the individual soul.

Some western Mystery schools or Orders have grades or degrees of attainment that are ranked into a number of divisions. There appear to be three major stages of individual development: Initiate, Adept and Priest. These stages are cumulative rather than serial.

Initiation means beginning. In the specialized sense that's intended here, the process of Initiation begins with a profound dissatisfaction with conventional wisdom and the exoteric doctrines of established religions. There are too many unanswered questions and inadequate answers in the major western religions, philosophies and life-ways. The Initiate seeks knowledge, and through knowledge, understanding, wisdom, and transformation.

Knowledge proceeds from the known to the unknown, so each of us begins with the basic facts of our own existence and experience. We know we were born into a line of ancestry that

recedes into prehistory. We are also aware of society around us, large numbers of our own species, each of whom has a unique world-view and personality.

We know that at some point in our life we will die, and what happens beyond death is a mystery. We know that we experience intangible events and facts. We can observe our own mentation and reactions; we accept the reality of such abstractions such as love, beauty, truth and spirit.

Our sense of art declares that our abilities and achievements should not be linked with our physical bodies in such a way as to share its destruction at death. We live a spiritual as well as a physical life. It is impossible to conceive of one's own extinction, even though we remember nothing prior to our early childhood. We accept a time without our presence, before we were born—but once having come into being, how can we not-be?

Our span of incarnation is finite, but our spirit is infinite. The sense of infinity creates the call to Initiation; answering that call is an act of joy.

We feel a growing certainty that there's more to life than meets the eye; more to living than we're taught in school, at home or in church. Determining to seek the Unknown is the first step of Initiation. Instinct leads us to books written by Initiates. We need to get a tangible entrance to our Path.

Initiated writings vary in their content and style. S o m e are complex and obscure, others are simple and lucid. Some books are written for the neophyte, others are more advanced.

One's intuition should be trusted in the selection of such reading material.

The beginner on the Path usually is attracted to a particular school or method, which he/she pursues to the point of self-development where other methods are studied for comparison and contrast. Initiates often become eclectic in search of those universal truths which underlie all effective schools, approaches, and methods.

The flow of the Magickal Current sometimes causes one to meet with living Initiates who are further along the path than one is. When one meets the correct Initiate, a learning situation occurs, with benefits in both directions. The elder Brother or Sister shares the fruits of experience, the younger shares a fresh point of view.

If the Current brings solitude at the beginning, one develops into a voracious reader, tracking down leads and references to further information. One searches out and finds occult shops, bookstores and groups of Initiates in the local environment.

It's not unusual for there to be peer-group blocs of Initiates in certain cities at certain times, who often find each other through occult shops. By peer-group bloc is meant a group of friends and acquaintances who share an interest in the occult sciences. These blocs often formalize their relationship or gestalt as a Coven, a Lodge, an Order, etc, for the purpose of sharing knowledge and performing group rituals.

Individuality is in no way compromised in the bloc; indeed,

Initiates are usually rugged individualists in the extreme, and the unity of the Great Work doesn't preclude lively debate.

It's recommended that Initiates who work solitary balance solitude with personal participation in the Brotherhood of Initiates. It's always a good idea to check one's Work with one's peers; at any level of Initiation one can become unbalanced in one's development. The love of the Brotherhood demands truth in all dealings. An opinion honestly asked is honestly given, courageously listened to, impartially judged, and if correct, applied.

Conversely, Initiates whose Work is mainly with a group should balance this activity with solitude in Temple, or better still, in the woods, fields, rivers, and mountains.

In Working with a group, we often operate in the state of no-mind, but more often in samadhi, a state of blissful non-personhood. We become involved in the situations and problems of our Sisters and Brothers, inasmuch as we're asked for, and give, advice. Sometimes this involvement can occupy all of our attention, and we lose sight of ourselves.

This is not a desirable loss, since our aim is to use everything we have and are in the Great Work. Self-awareness is necessary for the Will to control the self, to make sure all faculties, abilities, and strengths are at optimum operating levels. Time spent in solitary meditation and contemplation aids self-awareness.

The Initiate's search for truth usually leads through a series of Ordeals, or learning experiences. An Ordeal is an event or

condition that often involves pain, distress or tedium. The intensity of these factors depends on how strongly our behavior is contradicting our Will, on the time it takes for us to notice the contradiction and on the accuracy of our corrective action. A wise Initiate learns to anticipate Ordeals and make the needed self-corrections before the learning experience occurs. There is no virtue in pain.

One method of speeding the Initiation process is through practice of various disciplines and rituals, celebrating the Wheel of the Year and achieving an understanding of the principles underlying the practices.

When an Initiate achieves sufficient understanding through study and practice for generating his or her own rites, the level of Adept has been attained.

The performance of classical or traditional rituals is vital to the attainment of Adeptship. Just as painting students copy the works of the masters in order to place themselves in a creative condition similar to that of the masters, and to learn the secrets of the masters' techniques, so also does the Initiate re-create traditional rituals in order to place him/herself in a creative condition similar to that of the Adepts who generated and perfected the rituals, and to learn the secrets of those Adepts' techniques. Upon grasping the underlying principles of Magickal ritual, the Adept is enabled to create new and timely rites which are effective and efficient.

In a broad sense, Initiation deals with theory and knowledge, and Adeptship deals with practice. Of course, theory and

practice are mutually assisting. An Initiate practices and an Adept theorizes; the distinction is one of emphasis.

Aleister Crowley states that Magick unearthed is not Magick at all. When one realizes the true nature of the universe, the Self, and change, it is a natural progression to put this realization to use in "causing change to occur in conformity with Will."

The Initiate's Will is to learn; the Adept's Will is to do. One can only cease learning by adopting a blindness to events and their meaning. One can only cease doing by rendering one's actions chaotic and scattered.

There are dangers in Initiation and Adeptship.

A misplaced ego or domineering intellect can convince the Initiate that he/she has attained to the perfection of Art and need strive for excellence no longer. The uncontrolled force of emotion can cause either Initiate or Adept to act in ways contrary to his/her ethical realizations.

For the new Initiate-Adept, there is the danger of relying too heavily on the information or advice of the Elder Brother or Sister. At times it is possible for one to begin following a person rather than the Path, and fall into the trap of a "cult of personality." We see this often in the disciples of famous gurus. The disciples become a means of support, both financial and emotional, for the guru, and the guru becomes a substitute for self-responsibility. There is little difference between a follower of a living guru and a devotee of established religions with established priesthoods.

For those who are in the position of imparting information, there is the danger of becoming attached to the devotion of one's listeners. Respect and admiration from others is a slow poison, dangerous in the extreme.

It would seem obvious that those in a teaching position should be free of all attachments. One's responsibility toward one's listeners and to Truth is too great to give any place for the ego's wrongful manifestation.

It matters not about the status of teacher or listener; in Initiated communication, the only two factors that count are the truth of the matter being communicated, and the fact of communication itself. The latter is one major means of Intelligence's interlinking with Itself. Communicating, therefore, is a holy act, never to be profaned.

The Initiate, should he/she persevere in Initiation, eventually comes to live in a state of awe and reverence for the essential holiness of the universe. This holiness includes the Initiate; one's ethics derive from the truth of one's perceptions. One never blasphemes or degrades what one sees to be sacred.

The Adept operates from this awe as a wise Taoist. Increasingly, the Adept perceives his/her Will and Work as aligning with, and therefore becoming, the flow of things, the Magickal Current, the Tao. Action becomes easier as one approximates the natural course of events. One begins to perceive the natural course of events being diverted or delayed by those whose blindness to larger patterns causes them to act for short-term goals and local benefits.

Increasingly, the Adept's main function becomes that of removing obstacles to the manifestation of Tao-Teh. It seems to be that the only species capable of acting contrary to the flow of things is humanity—at least on this planet. Even demons follow natural law.

When the Initiate-Adept realizes that one's function consists of removing obstacles to Intelligence's reunion with Itself, when one perceives that opening the ways to Tao is necessary, sufficient and inevitable, then the Initiate-Adept arrives at the point of Priesthood.

A Priest is one who undertakes the responsibility of working in all possible ways for universal awakening, not ceasing until the reunion of Intelligence be completed. This same concept is phrased in the Boddhisattvic Vow: "I shall not cease from existence until every sentient being in the Universe is enlightened."

One presumes that anyone taking this Vow has attained to a certain level of enlightenment. Before a task can be undertaken, the need for that task must be perceived. Until we directly experience the unity of Intelligence, we are acting on faith and hope.

Virtues such as faith and hope are helpful to the Initiate in the beginning stages—for then we see through a glass, darkly; upon perceiving the necessity of the Vow, the Priest sees face to face. "Heaven" does not have to wait for death, but can be experienced in the flesh.

When one experiences the unity of Intelligence, one sees

that the fragments of Intelligence, which manifest as individual beings of all kinds, are already/still united with the universal Intelligence and thereby with each other. Intelligence is integral. Even though most individuals are not consciously aware of this unity, it nevertheless provides the ground of being for all, and all things participate in it.

It might be questioned concerning the need or desirability of universal enlightenment: if all things already do participate in the unity, why bother with the conscious awareness of unity?

The conscious awareness is part of the makeup of a sentient being. If that being does not hold the knowledge and experience of unity in its consciousness, that being is incomplete, imbalanced. Where the consciousness is ignorant of unity, difficulties and internal strife arise; action does not meet ethics, self-destructive behavior occurs, entire nations can be slaughtered, and general evil abounds.

It is impossible to cause enlightenment for another shard of universal Intelligence. The individual must reach the experience of unity on his/her own, although it is possible to offer hints and clues, to point to the direction in which this experience lies. The Priest assists others in preparing for this experience, but in no way can the Priest **give** the experience to another. Each individual is his/her own Messiah; "salvation" can be earned, but not granted.

The Truth of existence is ever-present; our perception and awareness of Truth grows with the passage of time. It is possible to see Truth whenever one has the capacity to do so:

that capacity of sight is achieved by the removal of the veils of illusion. One simple exercise in the removal of veils is this: try to locate yourself. Are you your name, or your position in the community? Are you your ancestry, your material possessions, your talents, skills, faults, defects or deeds? Are you your physical body, your mind, your emotions, your intuition, your creativity? (The onion layers we wear are being peeled away rapidly.) Are you your thoughts, your responses, your inspirations? Are you awareness, a point-of-view, a non-dimensional point? Can the eye see itself?

At the core of our individuality is the Nothing from which we came. In the words of the East, Atman, the core of the self, is Brahman, about which nothing true can be said and from which all things came. We **are** Intelligence.

Consider this proposal: all that is lives; all that lives is Intelligent. We recognize exoterically several levels of life: animal, vegetable, protozoan, bacterial, viral. Would it not be possible for there to be mineral Intelligence, thinking extremely slowly via crystal pressure-charges? Would it not be possible for there to be solar life, thinking by means of the plasma's convection currents? Would it not be possible for there to be subatomic life, thinking by means of the spins, charges, quantum-band shifts and traversing the matter-energy distinction?

Although Terran Priesthood is concerned with the evolution of **Homo sapiens** to **Homo veritas**, it aids the Work to become aware of the life/Intelligence of the universe and our place in it as individual and species. We have many new

friends to learn from and to teach, once we have achieved the condition of **Homo veritas**, unified Man, the Racial Unconscious expanded into Race Consciousness. Priestly responsibility is a joyful task as we live and work in total dedication to this transformation of humanity.

Intellectual agreement with the concept of the Priest's responsibility for universal enlightenment is not sufficient to sustain a lifetime of work and dedication. The vision of the unity of Intelligence must be experienced first-hand. This experience is attained by means of hard work and perserverence in the task of removing obstacles to the vision.

Mysticism and Magick are not contradictory; rather, they are two aspects of a single process. These aspects intertwine and reinforce each other, with no detailed pattern of order on an individual basis. The various schools of hidden teachings outline a common broad order of progress or evolution, but in practice, the steps and stages vary widely.

In brief review: the individual begins by experiencing a yearning for God, a desire for a more comprehensive understanding of the self, the universe, the way things work. The exoteric philosophies of tradition and established religions prove incapable of satisfying this yearning.

The individual seeks out sources of information, libraries, bookstores, accessible groups whose names imply knowledge of the hidden teachings. After a certain period of information intake, one begins to put the information into practice through various disciplines and rituals. The practices yield results—

"coincidences" manifest in the individual's life, results desired and unsuspected follow rituals, new and appropriate pieces of information become available; proof of the reality of Magick presents itself in unmistakable ways. In addition to interesting phenomena, rituals and disciplines open up new levels of perception through which further Initiations can occur.

As the individual progresses as an Initiate, he/she comes to recognize the universal laws governing effective Magickal practice, and eventually becomes able to design and perform new rites that work efficiently for him/herself and obliging colleagues. Sometimes the ideas for new rites and practices arrive in the mind as channelings, as though a higher intelligence is giving the ideas to the Adept. The identity of the source of ideas is irrelevant; the point is: do the ideas work when put into practice or not?

The subject matter of ritual practice evolves with the practitioner. In the beginning, much of one's practical Temple-work involves boons and blessings upon individuals or the world community at large. One does rituals for healing and health, for employment and financial well-being, for harmonious personal relationships, for peace, justice, famine relief, etc. Eventually one adds invocation and evocation, astral travel and rising on the planes.

Invocation is the calling upon of a godform to indwell in the caller, an effort to experience the nature of a particular god and to acquire from this a divine perspective as well as the particular powers of that god. Evocation is the calling upon of

a lower spirit—be it demon, elemental, or denizen of darkness—in order to understand its nature and to put the lower entity under the scrutiny and control of the mind and will.

Astral travel is a journey through Inner Space to realms inaccessible to the conscious mind and physical body, for the purpose of gaining information and control of events occurring at a distance or of events still in potentiality. One can encounter various types of astral entities during such travels; any information gained from them should be thoroughly tested before being accepted as true.

Rising on the planes is the practice of putting one's point-of-view in states of increasing lucidity and comprehension. One can rise on the planes rapidly or slowly, depending on one's own capacities and development. A good tool for this process is the Qabbalistic Tree of Life, a pattern of the microcosm and the macrocosm consisting of various Spheres and the Paths connecting them. With an intellectual grasp of the Tree, it's possible to create a spiritual environment conducive to the experience of a particular Sphere or Path.

All of these practices contribute to the growth of the individual's development, leading to the realization of Priesthood.

The Priest functions in a number of ways. Perhaps the most important function is that of the Priest as living talisman of the entire human race. The vow of responsibility forges a Magickal Link between the Priest and the rest of the species. This link, based on profound love, enhances the influence of

the Priest upon other people. As he/she lives and grows, so grows the spirituality of others. In a sense, the Priest is a pioneer, an explorer, a trailblazer. By accomplishing change within him/herself, the Priest opens the way for others to duplicate his/her accomplishments. Essentially, the opening of the way is achieved through direct talismanic action: i.e., doing something once, for the first time, makes it easier for it to be done again. Repeated accomplishment, especially if duplicated by other Priests, brings about the "hundredth monkey effect" in the race at large.

At the present writing, the human race does participate in the universal Intelligence through the "Racial Unconscious" as postulated by Jung. The talismanic link of the Priesthood operates through this Racial Unconscious as well as through the higher realms of pure spirit. Because of the deeper vision and greater power of the Priest, he/she has the ability to influence large numbers of his/her fellows; the influential flow from the mass of humanity to the Priest is of a lesser order, but is also real. There is a danger of falling back into a narrower and more primitive condition of reality should the Priest neglect his or her responsibilities of constant awareness and unflagging work.

The talismanic function obliges the Priest to strive for personal perfection at all times: the fate of the species depends on it. This does not mean, though, that the Priest should ever regard him/herself as a kind of Messiah or Savior, for such self-regard would reverse the effect of the Priestly work.

Many if not all writings on the hidden teachings emphasize the dangers of Ego, and speak of the need of undergoing "Ego-death" as a requirement for higher realms of consciousness. This death is not a destruction of the Ego as the sense of self, but a transformation and reordering of the Ego as part of the whole self. The virtue of humility is not a blind abasement of the self before a superior or supreme being; rather, humility is the vision of one's proper function in the universe, a correct judgment of one's successes and failures in fulfilling that function.

The Priest is not a Messiah or Savior; his or her function is not one of redemption or salvation, but of realization and evolution. A priest is a human among humans, motivated by enlightened self-interest. The sooner universal enlightenment is complete, the sooner the Priest will be free of the obligation of individual continuity and can resolve into pure undifferentiated Intelligence.

A second function of Priesthood is that of information-sharing. As mentioned earlier, the elder Brothers and Sisters share wisdom with the younger, the younger Brothers and Sisters share new points-of-view. At our present stage of evolution, the Priest shares information in ways suitable to his partners in dialogue.

Through his/her own experiments and experiences in self-knowledge, the Priest becomes ever more accurate at assessing the spiritual level of development of another person. From this assessment the Priest fashions and uses the most appropri-

ate persona or Mask, through which he/she communicates with the other person. The Priest seems familiar, compatible, comfortable; the other person relaxes and opens in receptivity.

When dealing with colleagues, there is no need of a Mask other than one's usual, everyday persona. At certain stages, Initiates may require one to use a Mask of extreme subtlety and power. ("Ye must teach, but ye may make severe the ordeals.") Sometimes Masks are used for play among Adepts and Priests; the only caveat for this is the power of the Mask to convince the wearer of the Mask's reality. The more skillfully crafted the Mask, the greater its power of conviction, especially if its reality is being reinforced through its relationships with other Masks in this play of Adepts.

It's a different matter when dancing the Mask with an uninitiate. Here one is employing a professional tool in a serious task: waking up a sleeper from his nightmares of fragmentation, dispersion and self-destruction. The concentration of the Priest's Will upon the task at hand keeps the Mask under control. A Mask is an artificial Ego created for the purpose of facilitating communication. In a sense it does have a life of its own because it is created and sustained from the Priest's own substance. At the core of each Mask is a point of identity, identical with the Priest's own point. The Priest is responsible for everything he/she creates or destroys.

Information-sharing can also occur through the practice of Art. One virtue of Art as a tool in the Great Work is its ability to move and change the audience through bypassing the verbal

censors of the unbalanced Ego. Art evokes response from the beholder. A good artist knows precisely which responses he/she wants to evoke, in what order and/or combination; he/she also has the skill to present the proper stimuli to accomplish it. Each medium of Art has its particular strengths and weaknesses.

Music can evoke emotional and spiritual responses. It communicates directly with our chakras; the precision and power of music's influence depends directly on the composer's and performer's genius. In the most sublime music, such as that of Bach and Beethoven, the evocation is of Intelligence itself and the ecstacy of the rapt listener.

Dance and mime evoke sympathy and relational openness from the audience. It also evokes admiration and awe of the human form in motion. As a species, we take pleasure in beauty, skill, grace, power and heart, all essential ingredients for the action-arts.

Graphic art, architecture and sculpture can evoke the entire spectrum of human response. The same holds true for still photography and motion pictures.

No matter what the medium, a talented Priest can communicate the great fact of our unity without preaching or didacticism. Art shows rather than tells. All great artists function as Priests, whether they think of themselves as Priests or not.

In addition to the talismanic and information-sharing functions, the Priest performs Temple-work as a ritualist in order to

augment sensitivity to the flow of the Magickal Current, to formally align his/her being with the Current, to add all the power and energy he/she is capable of channeling to the Current.

The Priest and the rest of the race participate in the actual generation of the Magickal Current. The collective electromagnetic energy of the human nervous system imparts a particular signature-signal on the carrier wave of the flow of time and universal energy. The force of our human signal returns amplified by its circuit of intergalactic space. Upon returning to Earth, the signal is received by all those with any degree of psychic sensitivity. The evolved signal is very attractive to those with clear vision. The sensitives begin to put the signal into practice, and the next pulse of the human signal is much stronger going in. Our physical/technological history grows exponentially, and so does the force of the evolved signal.

The ritualistic function of the Priesthood is as important as the other functions. A Priest's ritual technique differs from that of the Adept in that it is minimalist and often done in motionless silence.

A Priest gives advice when sincerely asked to do so, and has the right to intervene and comment whenever he/she sees fit. A Priest doesn't debate, argue, convince, or prove. A Priest speaks Truth in the most appropriate way possible, but doesn't try to sell his/her statements to anyone. Accepting or rejecting Truth when it's presented is the responsibility of the listener.

The Priest functions as spiritual counselor, healer of souls, speaker of truth. He/she is an explorer who returns to tell of high adventure and wondrous visions, then works to help all interested listeners to befit themselves for the journey. The Priest has experienced humanity's next step in evolution and from this experience works wholeheartedly for the rest of the race to take the step also.

The Priest functions as a warrior who battles restrictive dogmas in all their many guises. When appropriate, the Priest participates in and encourages the Outer political processes, doing whatever is possible to restructure the forms of society to better reflect the unity of Intelligence in the legislative process.

When our transformation is complete as a species, there will be no need for legislation, the state, national boundaries or artificial control of the flow of goods and services. There will be no need for armies, police, or prisons. The concept of wealth will be redefined; churches, corporations, charities and clubs based on exclusivity will be greatly changed or will disappear entirely.

In the meantime, the Priest exercises wisdom and creativity in using existing channels to assist the great leap humanity is facing. Paramaters of Priesthood vary with the situation and the individuals involved in it. To better enable oneself to work efficiently at all times, the Priest practices and continues to grow in knowledge, understanding, wisdom and silence. Any situation is best handled from the plane(s) above the plane in which it is occurring. This provides an overview from which to

see the situation in context, thus permitting the optimum resolution to be perceived.

By operating from the vantage of the Supernals (the Spheres of understanding, wisdom and silence), the Priest perceives and acts from the highest possible overview. Through habitual exercise, the Supernal view is maintained at all times—as an ideal situation. In practice, prevailing social attitudes insinuate themselves into any individual's thought processes, almost by osmosis, due to the sheer numbers of uninitiates in the world and the strength of their combined psychic fields. In order to combat the situation, it's helpful to design one's personal environment to remind one of the Supernal view, to engage in daily practice that reinforces the view, to carry on one's person an amulet or talisman to remind one of the Priestly office.

There is no such thing as resting on one's laurels or retirement in the Priesthood. It's truly a life's work, and more. Death itself is merely a short vacation —or sabbatical— that permits one to obtain a fresh and energetic vehicle through which to operate. An individual who has developed enough to see and embrace the Priesthood has also developed the strength of personal integration sufficient to survive intact through any number of deaths and births. To those who see personal survival as the antithesis of our course of returning to the Nothingness from whence we came, it might be said that personal dissolution cannot be complete until all are able to release their hold on illusion. The unity of Intelligence prevents selective dissolution.

The Priesthood's task is to make the unity of Intelligence obvious to the whole of the human race, so that this unity can also prevent the nightmare of nuclear annihilation. We live in a crucial time; each individual is responsible for our continuity and development. The Priesthood is the cadre of those who have fully accepted this responsibility.

Every facet of life participates in the work of the Priest. No ordinary motivation could inspire total dedication to such an enormous task. Only the experience of the unity of Intelligence, the experience of participating in the universal pattern of Consciousness can enable one to actually love one's neighbor as oneself. Our neighbor **is** ourself in the unity of Intelligence, and much of ourself is in pain through ignorance of this fact. There is nothing that is not of us. All that is we embrace in joyful recognition of our essential unity and identity.

The Priesthood is a condition of a soul on fire with love. "For I am divided for love's sake, for the chance of union."

6/16/85, Cincinnati, Ohio
Nema

About the Book

"The Priesthood is a condition of a soul on fire with love. The Priesthood is a way of life demanded by a certain level of spiritual responsibility, a way of life that focuses action and non-action toward universal enlightenment." Thus begins Nema's moving exposition on the position, responsibilities and rewards of the spiritual territory known as the "Priesthood." In this writing, she identifies the Priest as a living talisman of the entire human race, a pioneer, an explorer, a trailblazer. Through his/her own experimentations and experiences in self knowledge the Priest builds a formidable citadel of self knowledge crucial in bringing benefit to others. The text creates a net in which the Priesthood, and all of it connotations and denotations, is recaptured and placed squarely again within the context of our living, magickal community.

About the Author

Nema encountered the works of Aleister Crowley in the early 1970s and became a member of Kenneth Grant's Typhonian Order for several years. During the same time period, she practiced group rituals with other magickians in Cincinnati, Ohio, and became a member of Bate Cabal, publisher of the *Cincinnati Journal of Ceremonial Magick*.

Nema is an experienced magickian and mystic, and the author of *Maat Magick* and *The Way of Mystery* (republished by Black Moon Publishing as *Wings of Rapture*). She is an Elder and High Priestess of the Circle of the Sacred Grove, Church of Pantheist Wicca, and an initiate of Adi Nath Tantra. She and her husband Lyrus live in southeastern Ohio, in the foothills of the Appalachian mountains. Nema is a founding member of the Horus-Maat Lodge and may be contacted via the HML website at horusmaat.com.